Lisa Leslie

Slam Dunk Queen

SPORTS LEADERS

Lisa Leslie

Slam Dunk Queen

Jeff Savage

Enslow Publishers, Inc.

40 Industrial Road   PO Box 38
Box 398   Aldershot
Berkeley Heights, NJ 07922   Hants GU12 6BP
USA   UK

http://www.enslow.com

Library of Congress Cataloging-in-Publication Data

Savage, Jeff, 1961–
    Lisa Leslie : slam dunk queen / Jeff Savage.— 1st ed.
        p. cm. — (Sports leaders)
    Includes bibliographical references and index.
    ISBN 0-7660-2423-7
    1. Leslie, Lisa, 1972–   —Juvenile literature. 2. Basketball players—United
States—Biography—Juvenile literature. I. Title. II. Sports leaders series
GV884.L47S38   2005
796.323'092—dc22

                                        2004012152

Printed in the United States of America

10 9 8 7 6 5 4 3 2 1

Illustration Credits: Adam Pretty/Allsport, p. 87; Allen Einstein/WNBAE via Getty Images, p. 12; Andrew D. Bernstein/WNBAE via Getty Images, p. 23; Andrew D. Bernstein/WNBAE/Getty Images, p. 82; Courtesy of the University of Southern California, pp. 18, 21, 26, 29, 36, 38, 43, 45, 50, 54; Doug Pensinger/Getty Images, p. 60; Frazer Harrison/Getty Images, p. 75; Gregory Shamus/WNBAE via Getty Images, p. 14; Harry How/Allsport, p. 90; Harry How/Getty Images, p. 77; Jed Jacobsohn/Getty Images, pp. 62, 67; Jesse D. Garrabrant/WNBAE via Getty Images, p. 10; Mark Morrison/ Getty Images, p. 80; Noah Graham/WNBAE/Getty Images, p. 84; Ray Amati/WNBAE via Getty Images, p. 32; Rick Stewart/Allsport, p. 65; Todd Warshaw/Getty Images, p. 72; Tom Pidgeon/Getty Images, p. 6.

Cover Illustration: Ray Amati/WNBAE via Getty Images.

CONTENTS

A
CHAPION

Lisa Leslie kept cool and focused. Eight minutes had been played in the game, and she still had not scored a point. Her Los Angeles Sparks were clinging to an 11–10 lead over the Detroit Shock in the opening game of the 2003 Women's National Basketball Association (WNBA) Finals. Other players would have been frustrated with the situation. Leslie simply concentrated and stayed on task.

Leslie knew the Sparks needed to win this game. The final two games of the best-of-three series would be played on Detroit's home court. The two teams had played in Detroit once during the regular season, and the Sparks lost, 87–78, in overtime.

In that game, the Shock overcame a 16-point deficit, then outscored Los Angeles 11–2 in overtime. The Sparks finished the season with a 24–10 record. The Shock finished 25–9, one game better. Because of their better record, the Shock had the homecourt advantage in the playoffs.

With a sold-out Staples Center crowd and millions of television viewers watching, Leslie seized control. She gathered in a rebound at the defensive end and flipped the ball to Nikki Teasley. She raced down the court, took a return pass from Teasley, rose up, and drilled an 18-footer. The Shock responded with a basket to cut the lead back to one. Leslie tried to answer, but her short jumper missed. Teammate DeLisha Milton grabbed the offensive rebound but missed the put-back. Leslie crashed the boards and hauled in Milton's miss. Leslie went up over Ruth Riley to put the ball in off the glass. At the other end, Kedra Holland-Corn threw a pass that Leslie smartly stole. Leslie whipped the ball to Milton, who fed Tamecka Dixon for the basket and a five-point lead. Timeout Shock.

Now Leslie was playing the way everyone knew

> Other players would have been frustrated. . . . Leslie simply concentrated and stayed on task.

she could. Leslie was widely considered the best female basketball player in the world. The Sparks were the two-time defending WNBA champions, and Leslie was the main reason why. In these 2003 playoffs, the Sparks rolled through the Minnesota Lynx and Sacramento Monarchs to reach the finals again. When Sacramento coach John Whisenant watched Leslie almost single-handedly eliminate his Monarchs, he said, "Lisa Leslie is the Shaquille O'Neal of the WNBA. She is both an offensive and defensive threat. She is a handful."[1]

But the Shock were young and hungry. Most experts and fans agreed that the Sparks would not have as easy a time in the finals as they did the two previous years when they swept the Charlotte Sting and New York Liberty to win the crown. Detroit's front line was taller and bigger than the Sparks's. Swin Cash, Detroit's leading scorer, stood six feet two inches. Cheryl Ford, the WNBA Rookie of the Year and daughter of NBA superstar Karl Malone, was six feet three inches. Center Ruth Riley was the same height as Leslie, six feet five inches. The difference was that Riley was 25 pounds heavier. Ford also weighed 50 pounds more than her counterpart, Sparks forward Mwadi Mabika.

"They're probably going to try to beat up on us,

Lisa Leslie snatches away a loose ball from the Detroit Shock's Barbara Farris during the 2003 WNBA Finals.

lean on us," said Leslie. "I can't put on 20 or 30 pounds in the next day or so. I have to play to my advantage, and that's being faster and obviously trying to outsmart the post players."[2]

Leslie's favorite phrase is "Let's go for the jugular."[3] She and her teammates did just that, choking off the Shock on offense over the next eight minutes as they went on a 21–4 run to put away the game. It began innocently, with a free throw by Dixon and a layup by Milton. Then Leslie threw a sharp pass to

Dixon, who hit a 14-foot jumper. After Deanna Nolan answered with a basket for the Shock, Dixon drilled a three-pointer to give the Sparks an eleven-point lead, 25–14. Leslie increased the margin on her team's next possession by nailing a 12-foot jumper. When Vanessa Nygaard drained a three-pointer and Milton hit a short jumper, Detroit coach Bill Laimbeer desperately called another timeout. Laimbeer had played on championship teams with the Detroit Pistons in the 1980s. In a memorable NBA Finals in 1988, Laimbeer's team was beaten by the Los Angeles Lakers. Leading the Lakers defense that year was veteran Michael Cooper. Now, fourteen years later, Cooper was squaring off with Laimbeer again, as coach of the Sparks.

As a former center, Laimbeer knew the importance of controlling the inside area of the basket. He could see that Ruth Riley was unable to stop Leslie by herself. Laimbeer switched his defense from man-to-man to a zone, so that Riley could get help from her frontcourt mates, Cash and Ford. It did not matter. After Cash made a layup following the time-out, Leslie scored the next three baskets. First, she rose up over Riley to hit a soft 9-foot jump shot. Next, she went over Riley and Ford to pop a 13-foot jumper. Finally, she drained a 16-footer to push the

Lisa Leslie defends against Cheryl Ford of the Detroit Shock during Game 2 of the 2003 WNBA Finals.

score to 38–16. The crowd in Los Angeles was on its feet now, well aware that the Sparks were on their way to taking Game 1. Moments later, the half ended with the score 42–21, the second-largest halftime lead in WNBA history.

After the game, Leslie was asked about her matchup with Riley. She told reporters, "I don't think she can guard me at all. That's the reason why they went to a zone."[4] It seemed like a bold statement to make, but to those who know Leslie, it is her supreme confidence that makes her great. Away from basketball, she is gentle, soft-spoken, and likes to read romance novels. She also has a second job—as a model. Working for a modeling agency, she does photo shoots for commercials and models lovely outfits. She calmly walks down the runway, wearing four-inch heels, an elegant evening gown, and a radiant smile.

But as a basketball player, she pounds down the court in her purple and yellow uniform like a relentless bulldog, sweating, scowling. "It's like this Wonder Woman thing," Leslie says. "I'm the most polite person you'll ever meet off the court. But I put on my uniform and . . . what can I say? My hair's a mess. I'm yelling. I don't care. Don't mess with my teammates, don't mess with me. I want to win."[5]

Lisa Leslie shoots over Ruth Riley during Game 3 of the WNBA Finals on September 16, 2003, at the Palace of Auburn Hills in Michigan.

It is almost as though Leslie is two different people. How can she switch back and forth from elegant model to ferocious athlete? "When it's time to play," she says, "something clicks in my mind, and I become . . . almost like a monster."[6]

The second half of the game was as easy as riding in a parade. As the Staples Center crowd cheered, the Sparks cruised to an easy win. Detroit scored the first six points of the half, but the Sparks scored the next four and never let the Shock get closer than 12 points, the final margin of the game. With the 75–63 victory, the Sparks were one win away from their third straight WNBA crown. The WNBA began in 1997 with the Houston Comets winning the first four titles. Then Leslie and the Sparks took over. Would they become the next dynasty? The teams were headed to Detroit to find out.

2

GROWING UP FAST

Lisa Deshaun Leslie was born July 7, 1972. She grew up in Inglewood, California. Inglewood was where the Los Angeles Lakers played their home basketball games, and most of the town's residents were crazy about basketball. But not Lisa. In fact, there was a time when she hated the game.

Lisa's father, Walter, walked out on the family when Lisa was two months old. Christine Leslie, Lisa's mother, had to raise Lisa and her seven-year-old sister, Dionne, by herself. Walter occasionally sent the family a little money, but he was never a part of their life. Lisa saw him just once after he left. Lisa was twelve years old when Walter died.

Although her height made her a natural basketball player, Lisa Leslie was slow to take up the game.

Christine always tried to be a positive influence on her daughters. She often told Lisa, "If you don't touch the moon, at least you can catch a star."[1] Lisa's nickname was "The Shadow" because she always followed her mother around their home.

When Lisa began attending elementary school, she noticed that she was taller than her classmates. In second grade she was a head taller than her 5-foot-2-inch teacher. Lisa thought it was cool being the tallest person in the classroom. Later, she would resent her height.

At home, Lisa's mother conducted "etiquette classes" for her daughters. She taught them proper table manners, told them to not flop on the couch, and insisted that they stand tall as they walked. Lisa began to like the idea of someday becoming a model. She noticed on television that models walked smoothly down the runway in their fancy outfits, their heads barely moving. Lisa learned to walk this way by putting books on her head and walking around the house. Lisa's mother was encouraging. She would put on some music and wait in her bedroom, holding a hairbrush like a microphone. Lisa would announce that she was ready, and then she would walk carefully down the hallway and into her mother's room. "Here comes Lisa," her mother would announce into the hairbrush, "wearing her blue-jean skirt and butterfly collar shirt!"[2]

Money was tight for the Leslies. Lisa's mother worked hard as a postal worker. But when Lisa was nine, Christine learned that some employees at the post office would soon be losing their jobs. Rather than wait around, Christine took action. She began driving a truck! She bought an 18-wheeler to make long hauls across the country. As it turned out, being a trucker was both good and bad for the family. The good news was that Christine was able to earn more money. The bad news was that she was away from home for long stretches of time.

By now, Lisa had a little sister, Tiffany. When Christine was on the road, the three girls were cared for by different adults. For a time, a live-in house-keeper stayed with the girls. Later, the girls lived nearby with an aunt. During a three-year stretch from 1982 to 1985, Lisa lived in three different homes and attended four different schools. Naturally, Lisa had difficulty adjusting. Sometimes she held a framed picture of her mother and cried herself to sleep. At school, she did her best to hide her tears. "I cried all day wishing my mom was home," she said.[3]

Lisa was responsible for making sure her little sister had dinner. She said it helped her mature more

During one three-year stretch of her childhood, Lisa Leslie lived in three different homes and attended four different schools. Lisa had a difficult time adjusting to all this moving around.

quickly. Today, Lisa reflects on this difficult period of her childhood as positive. "My mom taught me the importance of responsibility and hard work," she says. "Struggle is good, and that's part of life."[4] Still, Lisa could not wait until summertime when school would let out. She and her sisters would join their mother on cross-country trips in the 18-wheeler. They would eat at roadside diners, buy school clothes in different towns along the route, and sleep in a narrow bed in back of the truck's cab.

By the time she reached the fifth grade, Lisa had become embarrassed about being so tall. Her class-mates teased her. They called her "skinny bones" or "Olive Oyl," after the character in *Popeye* cartoons. Lisa would run home crying. Her mother would try to comfort her. "Enjoy who you are," Christine would say. "Be tall and proud of it."[5]

Christine, who grew to six feet three inches in height, would tell Lisa how she, too, was teased when she was young. Christine explained that she did not let the taunts stop her, and now she was doing "a man's job," driving a truck, yet she kept her hair and nails beautiful, looking every bit a woman. Lisa says now that eventually her mother's encour-agement did wonders. "The closer I grew to my mother's height," Lisa said, "the more beautiful I

By the fifth grade, Lisa Leslie had to endure teasing for being so tall. In time, she would learn to embrace her height.

felt."[6] Lisa learned smart and honest replies to the cruel comments. "Yeah, I'm tall," she would say. "Yep, my feet are big." Today, she explains, "They teased me then, and now my feet make me money."[7]

Christine came through for Lisa in other ways, too. One time, when Lisa's fifth-grade class was given a show-and-tell assignment, Lisa brought her mother and her 18-wheeler to school. Christine parked the long truck in front of the school, and the students got to climb inside. "I became very popular after that," Lisa said.[8]

By sixth grade, Lisa already stood six feet tall. Because of her height, it was expected that she would play basketball. People constantly asked her if she played the game. She grew tired of the same question over and over again. Eventually, she became defensive. "I didn't want to play basketball at first," Lisa later explained, "because everyone assumed that I would play, since I'm tall."[9]

Lisa hated the game. In fact, she had no interest in sports. Her dream was to be a model or a weather reporter.

3

LEARNING
THE GAME

Sharon Hargrove was the best basketball player at Lisa's junior high school. Sharon convinced Lisa to start playing the game, at least outside on the playground. At first, Lisa was afraid of getting hurt. "I cannot handle falling out here on this concrete," she said to herself.[1]

Lisa's mother was delighted to hear that her daughter was at least trying to enjoy the game. Christine told Lisa that her father was once a great outdoor basketball player in the neighborhood. Christine thought Lisa needed to know about her father. "It was important for her to feel she had a

Lisa Leslie huddles together with her college teammates. Leslie first took up playing basketball in junior high.

father," said Christine, "even if it was only in her own mind."[2]

Lisa began to feel the thrill of putting the basketball in the hoop. With her height, she could jump and grab rebounds. She liked controlling the ball beneath the basket. She joined her school team soon after, playing center. The team went undefeated, winning all seven of its games. Lisa figured that maybe playing basketball was not so bad after all.

Lisa was feeling better about herself and her height. She decided to pursue the game further. While she was aware that she dominated shorter opponents because of her height, she did not fool herself. She knew that if she was going to play basketball seriously, she needed to improve her skills to compete against better players. She sought help from her cousin, Craig.

Lisa had been living with her aunt and Craig that year. Craig knew how to play the game. Together Lisa and Craig practiced at the neighborhood basketball courts. Craig taught Lisa post-up moves and how to handle the ball in the open court. He was tough on her, demanding that she make the right moves and play the game correctly. Lisa did pushups and sit-ups to get in top shape. She played in pick-up games at the playground to improve her skills. Lisa was driven to become great. "I've always listened to what anybody has told me and then I'd work hard," she explained. "There's so much to learn. I'm not one to say, 'Oh, isn't this enough? Can't I stop?' You can never learn enough."[3]

In eighth grade, Lisa played in an all-boys league called Slam-n-Jam. Often the boys would not pass Lisa the ball. There was only one way for Lisa to get it. "I stole the ball from my own teammates," she admitted.[4]

When Lisa enrolled at Morningside High School as a fourteen-year-old freshman, she stood six feet three inches tall. She loved competing in sports now, and so she played on the girls' volleyball team in the fall. She made it clear, though, that her main focus would be basketball. When the volleyball season ended and the basketball season began, Lisa told coach Frank Scott of her desire to be a great basketball player. Coach Scott was prepared to help. "When Lisa came here, she was green," said the coach. "She was a little clumsy, a little awkward on the court. She'd keep me overtime. But I didn't mind at all. I saw the potential."[5]

Each day after practice Lisa and Coach Scott worked on fundamental drills. They repeated each move over and over. Lisa yearned for perfection.

By the time she began her freshman year of high school, Lisa had developed a great love of playing sports, participating in both basketball and volleyball.

This attitude separated her from other tall girls with similar potential. Before her first game as a freshman, Lisa was named the team's starting center. She was thrilled. Over the next four years, the Lady Monarchs would play 134 games. Lisa was the starting center for every one of them. She led her team to the Ocean League title as a freshman, and along the way she threw down her first dunk. She did it in pre-game warm-ups, but that did not matter to the fans in the bleachers, who gasped in amazement. A fourteen-year-old freshman dunking on a regulation ten-foot rim? *A girl?*

> "You can never learn enough."
>
> —Lisa Leslie

One day during her freshman year, Lisa acted in a school play. She played Olympic track star Wilma Rudolph. She ran as fast as she could around the school auditorium. "The track coach saw my performance," Lisa said, "and put me on the track team!"[6] Lisa would soon become a champion high jumper. By Lisa's sophomore year, she was smartly preparing for college by getting excellent grades. She had become so popular that her schoolmates voted her class president.

On the basketball court, she patterned her style of play after star forward James Worthy of the Los Angeles Lakers. "I loved to watch James because he was a go-to player," said Lisa. "Whenever the Lakers needed a basket in a big game, they would give it to 'Big Game James.' When I'd watch him, I'd say, 'One day I want to be that kind of player.'"[7] Lisa led the Lady Monarchs to another league title and then a California Southern Section title. She was named to the 1988 California Interscholastic Federation (CIF) First Team.

Lisa was voted class president again her junior year. She led Morningside to the Southern CIF section title. With Lisa dominating underneath the basket, the Lady Monarchs cruised all the way to the California state championship. She was an easy choice for the CIF First Team again, and this time she was honored as one of the best girl basketball players in the country by being selected to the *Parade* All-America team.

As a senior, Lisa would win these same awards and so much more. During the summer before her senior year, she played on the Junior World Championship team. She showcased her talents to college recruiters throughout the country, and by the time school began again in the fall, she had become the most heavily-recruited high school player in the country. She made time to serve as class president for a third year, and she studied extra hard

Lisa Leslie soars to the hoop. Leslie first began dunking the ball while still only a high school freshman.

for college, earning As and Bs. She even played on the volleyball team again, and she was named to the All-Ocean League team. But Lisa had her sights set on basketball.

Lisa had a remarkable senior season. She was unstoppable on the court, and sometimes she even dunked in games, just for the fun of it. She averaged more than 27 points and 15 rebounds per game, numbers especially impressive since Coach Scott often took her out of games at halftime to give her teammates more playing time. Lisa's ability drew so much attention from newspapers around the country that as the season came to an end, the Lady Monarchs were ranked number two in the nation.

Lisa closed out the season in a memorable way. For Morningside's final game each year, it was a tradition to let the senior captain try to score as many points as possible. The underclassmen would get the rebounds and pass the ball to that senior. Lisa's turn came against the South Torrance High Spartans. Lisa got the ball and put it in the basket. The Lady Monarchs stole the ball, passed it to Lisa, and she scored again. Then she scored another basket, and then another. The Spartans could see what was happening. They double-teamed her. They triple-teamed her. They even quadruple-teamed her.

But they could not stop her. Lisa made layups, hook shots, jump shots, everything. After the first quarter, she had scored 49 points!

When the players came over to the bench between quarters, Lisa was in a daze. "I thought it was already halftime," Lisa said. "I didn't know what was going on."[8]

The second quarter was more of the same. The Lady Monarchs pressed on defense and stole the ball often, then fed it in to Leslie for yet another basket. The halftime score was 102–24. Lisa had scored 52 more points in the second quarter, for a total of 101 points! One other Morningside player scored, but only a point. Lisa had made 37 of 56 shots from the floor and 27 of 35 free throws. She was only five points away from the all-time girls' national high school record. In 1982, Cheryl Miller of Riverside Poly High School in California had scored 105 points. But that was in a *game*. Lisa had scored 101 points in a *half*.

> "One day I want to be that kind of [big-game] player."
>
> —Lisa Leslie

During halftime, South Torrance made an astonishing announcement. The Spartans were not going to play the second half. They were going to forfeit the game. South Torrance explained that it could not even put five players on the court for the second half. The Spartans had seven players to start the game, but two had fouled out, and one was now injured, so they were down to four players. They refused to play the second half. Lisa would not get to break the national scoring record.

The referees thought it was unfair that Lisa would not be allowed a chance to break the record, and so they charged South Torrance with four technical fouls. This gave Morningside four free throw attempts before the game would be declared over. Lisa stepped to the free throw line and made all four free throws to tie Cheryl Miller's record. Unfortunately, these four points were later disallowed by conference officials, who explained that the game was officially over the moment South Torrance forfeited. Still, Lisa's performance captured the imagination of people everywhere. Suddenly, she was a star.

After the game, Lisa went to eat dinner at a restaurant with her teammates. When she got home that night, she was besieged with phone calls. "Everybody was looking for me," she said. "Every TV channel from 2 to 13, every newspaper. I didn't know it was that big."[9]

By the next day, the news had traveled nationwide. It was reported the same way everywhere:

In the final game of her senior season, Lisa Leslie challenged the all-time girls' national high school record for points in a game, set by Cheryl Miller (above).

Girl basketball player scores 101 points—in one half!
Some fans and sportswriters criticized Lisa for trying
to rack up points against an inferior opponent. They
said such a scoring fest showed poor sportsmanship.
Lisa was hurt by the criticism. She defended herself,
saying it was all in the spirit of competition. "It
wasn't personal. They knew I was going for the
record," Lisa explained. "I wasn't trying to rub anybody's nose in the dirt. I was only trying for the
record."[10]

With Lisa leading the way, Morningside High
rolled through the playoffs to reach the state final
for the second straight year. Along the way, Lisa
dominated the competition with performances such
as the Southern Section title game, where she
finished with 29 points, 23 rebounds, and 12 blocked
shots. In the state title game against Berkeley
High, however, the situation appeared bleak for the
Lady Monarchs. Lisa was ill. She had a 103-degree
temperature and a severe case of chicken pox. Still,
she insisted on playing. She did not want to let her
teammates down.

With a large crowd at the Oakland Arena watching,
Lisa scored 35 points, grabbed 12 rebounds, and
blocked 7 shots to lead the Lady Monarchs to a 67–56
victory. Lisa's team had won its second consecutive

After a brilliant high school and college career, Cheryl Miller would go on to a very successful career as a women's basketball coach.

state title. Afterward, while her teammates went out to celebrate, Lisa went straight to the hospital. "I don't even remember the game," Lisa says now. "All I remember is lying in that hospital bed, getting blood drawn, getting shots. I didn't even get to go to the championship party."[11]

Lisa won nearly every national player of the year trophy, including the prestigious awards sponsored by Gatorade, *USA Today*, and Naismith. In Lisa's four years at Morningside High, she led her basketball team to a combined record of 125–9, including 28–2 in the playoffs. She scored 2,856 points, the second-most in California history, and she grabbed 1,705 rebounds—the most ever in the state.

In the spring, Lisa ended her high school experience with a flourish by winning her second straight state high jump title in track. Now Lisa was ready to make her next leap—to college.

RECORD BREAKER

Lisa Leslie was wanted by nearly every university in the country that had a good women's basketball team. Because of her basketball skills and her 3.5 grade-point average in high school, she knew that she could live almost anywhere in the United States. Leslie decided to live ten minutes from home.

The University of Southern California was just a short drive up the freeway from her house in Inglewood. USC did not have a major powerhouse women's basketball program. The Trojans had finished just 8–19 a year earlier. But Leslie wanted her mother to be able to see her play. When she informed USC coach Marianne Stanley of her choice, Stanley was thrilled. "I felt better than a Lotto winner," said the coach. "You can keep the million bucks, I'll take Lisa!"[1]

Before Leslie joined her Trojans teammates, she spent part of the summer of 1990 with the best women's basketball players in the country. She had joined them at the University of South Florida to try to make the United States national team. The best 12 players would form the team that would compete later that summer in the World Championships in Malaysia and the Goodwill Games in Seattle, Washington. "This is a great opportunity for her," said national team coach Teresa Grentz. "We're talking about going against players who are technically professionals. It will be an eye-opening experience for her."[2] The group traveled to Cuba to play a pair of games and then was pared down to 13 players. Leslie was still among them. She was easily the youngest of the group. Then the final player to be cut was announced. It was Leslie. She was disappointed for a moment, but she quickly realized that she would have many chances to represent the United States in basketball. She returned to Southern California to prepare for her first season with USC.

Other college coaches from the area had seen Leslie play in high school. They knew what they

Lisa Leslie grabs a rebound.

were up against. Cal State Long Beach coach Joan Bonvicini, who almost persuaded Leslie to attend her college, said, "She's one of the best athletes I've seen and potentially could be the best player ever."[3] UCLA coach Billie Moore said, "You don't work trying to stop someone like that. We might have to tackle her at half court or something like that."[4] But Trojans coach Stanley cautioned everyone that Leslie had not accomplished anything in college—yet. "People are expecting a lot, but how good Lisa is going to be remains to be seen," said coach Stanley. "Suffice it to say, she has vast potential. She can be as good as anyone who's played the game."[5]

Leslie had now reached her full height of six feet five inches. She was USC's starting center from the beginning. If there was any doubt about how she would perform in college, that doubt was eliminated in her very first game. The Trojans opened the season at the Los Angeles Sports Arena against the University of Texas. The Longhorns were ranked seventh in the country and had whipped USC 85–44, the year before. The Trojans had lost their leading scorer and leading rebounder from that team to graduation. So, how badly would they be pummeled by Texas this time? With Leslie leading the way, USC was an entirely different team. Leslie

Lisa Leslie defends an inbounds pass.

pounded the Longhorns in the paint as she scored 30 points and grabbed 20 rebounds. The Trojans upset the Longhorns 88–77. "I'll tell you, to see her step up in her first game against Texas and take charge was really something," said coach Stanley afterward.[6] "I've never seen a better debut by anyone I've ever coached."[7]

After splitting two games in a tournament at Northwestern University, the Trojans returned home to face San Diego State. With Leslie clogging the middle on defense, the Trojans held the Aztecs scoreless for the first five minutes of the game and jumped out to a 12–0 lead. Leslie made it even worse for the Aztecs in the second half as she helped shut them out for the first 12 minutes. USC built up a 53–33 lead and then cruised to a 68–54 victory. Leslie hauled in 23 rebounds and added 20 points. Her rebound total fell one shy of the USC single-game record, set in 1984 by Cheryl Miller. The Trojans dropped their next three games but then set sail on a six-game winning streak to run their record to 9–5. In an 88–74 win over Arizona, Leslie scored 30 points and swatted away 6 shots.

"She's one of the best athletes I've seen and potentially could be the best player ever."

—Coach Joan Bonvicini

Her 6 blocks were a Pac-10 Conference season high. Facing the talented University of California Bears in Berkeley, Leslie did all she could to keep USC's winning streak alive. But the Trojans lost in a heart-breaker 92–86. Leslie's 33 points were the most she would score all season. Later in the year, she scored 32 to lead USC to a 69–62 upset of No. 9 ranked Washington. Along the way, Leslie was having fun on the court with something else, too—the dunk.

In the mid-1980s, Georgiana Wells of the University of West Virginia had been the only player to ever dunk in a women's college game. Leslie gained fame by occasionally slamming the ball down through the rim. But Leslie said that the move was not particularly safe because women players were not used to being dunked on and they could accidentally undercut her. She did most of her dunking during pre-game warm-ups. "It's not that big of a deal for me, but if it brings more attention to the women's game, then great," Leslie said. "Dunking is something guys care about more than girls. There is something about jumping that seems to fascinate guys."[8]

The Trojans qualified for the National Collegiate Athletic Association (NCAA) Tournament and beat Utah 63–52 in the first round. But their season ended three days later in an NCAA West Regional contest with an 83–58 drubbing at the hands of Cal State Long Beach. Still, the season was quite a turnaround from the year before, as USC finished with an overall record of 18–12. Leslie led all other freshmen in the country in scoring at 19.4 points and 10 rebounds per game, making her an easy choice as the National Freshman of the Year. She also became the first freshman ever named to the conference's All-PAC 10 team.

Leslie and the Trojans soared in her sophomore year, going 23–8 on the season and getting deeper in the NCAA Tournament. Along the way, Leslie scored her 1,000th point while racking up 32 points against Cal. But Leslie did not care about personal accomplishments as much as she did winning. After the game, she was more excited that her team upset Cal with a 68–62 victory. The Trojans fared worse against their other Bay Area nemesis, Stanford—a team they had not beaten in four years. In a conference game against the Stanford Cardinal in January, USC was defeated 87–72. Cardinal center Val Whiting pounded Leslie inside to score a career-high 35 points and grab nine rebounds. Leslie's 25 points and six rebounds were a fine effort but paled in comparison. "She uses her body very well," Leslie said about Whiting. "She banged me and tried to move me back toward the basket. She's very good."[9]

Exactly one month later, Whiting and Stanford beat USC again, this time by 18 points. In the NCAA tournament, the Trojans defeated Montana and Stephen F. Austin to reach the second round of the West Regional. Their next opponent was Stanford. Once again, Leslie's team was overpowered by Whiting and the Cardinal, this time by 20 points. Leslie finished the season with more blocked shots than anyone else in the conference. She was a second-team All-America selection and was the only sophomore selected as a semifinalist for the Naismith College Player of the Year award. Despite the honors, Leslie knew she had more to work on, especially defense.

Leslie trained hard during the off-season. She lifted weights to increase her strength. She learned more moves from coach Stanley. She

Leslie did not care about personal accomplishments as much as she did winning.

shot countless baskets in the gym. When her team met Stanford again midway through her junior season, she was ready. The Cardinal were the defending NCAA champions when they arrived at the Lyon Center on USC's campus. What's more, they had all

Lisa Leslie tries to defend the jump shot of Stanford's Val Whiting.

five returning starters, including Val Whiting. Both teams were unbeaten in conference play, but USC had lost 10 straight games to the Cardinal. This outcome would be different.

With Leslie and Whiting banging against one another down low, Stanford took an early 13–9 lead. But USC answered with six straight points. Stanford took the lead again by a single point, 18–17, but it would be their last lead of the night. The Trojans went on an 8–1 run that put them ahead for good. Leslie scored six points down the stretch as USC took a 37–24 lead at the half. In the second half, USC kept its distance, never letting the Cardinal get closer than seven points. Leslie led a smothering defense as the Trojans won the game 67–55. Leslie celebrated with her teammates in an emotional group hug on the court. The 55 points were Stanford's lowest output in a game in six years. Leslie tallied 27 points and 14 rebounds to lead the Trojans. Even more impressive, she frustrated Whiting, limiting the Stanford star to just 6-of-17 shooting from the floor. "I did everything I was asked to do," said Leslie, "for the first time."[10]

The Trojans finished the season 22–8 and were eliminated after two games in the NCAA Tournament. Their final ranking of 15th in the nation was Leslie's highest, and her usual list of awards followed, including All-America and finalist for the Naismith award. She was also named the USA Basketball Player of the Year.

As a senior, Leslie would become the first player ever to be selected to the All-PAC-10 team all four years. But her achievements in the 1993–94 season would be far greater. Cheryl Miller had taken over as coach of the team. USC won its last national title in 1986 when Miller was a player on the team. Leslie was joined inside by freshman Tina Thompson. Together they formed a formidable duo. The Trojans roared to a 6–0 start. By the middle of February their record was 17–1. Their only loss was to Iowa by a single point. Leslie used her finesse and shooting ability to take over games on offense. She dominated on defense with her shot blocking and quickness. She scored more than 30 points in four contests. None was more impressive than her performance at the Lyon Center in a game against mighty Stanford.

> "I did everything I was asked to do for the first time."
>
> —Lisa Leslie

Before the opening tip, coach Miller pulled Leslie aside and told her to "just have fun."[11] Leslie was having a blast when the Trojans jumped out to a huge 17–2 lead in the first eight minutes of the game. Leslie had scored seven points to lead the charge. But the Cardinal fought back to close within two points at the half, 38–36. The teams ping-ponged back and forth in the second half, and with 11:28 left, the Cardinal surged ahead by six, 57–51. USC rallied to tie it 59–59. Then Leslie took over.

She made a layup to give her team the lead and start a 12–2 run. Nearly four minutes later, she made another layup to cap the run and put the Trojans up 71–61. She nailed four free throws in the final minute to preserve the win 81–73. Leslie had finished with 34 points—her career high. "Lisa Leslie showed why she is the best player out there," said coach Miller. "She was tremendous."[12]

The Trojans lost twice more in the regular season, and one of those defeats was a rematch at Stanford. Speaking to newspaper reporters after that loss, coach Miller guaranteed that her team would not lose another game. It was a bold statement, but Miller could not help being confident. After all, she had the best college player in the nation. And her prediction nearly came true.

The Trojans were 23–3 and ranked No. 7 in the country as they opened play in the NCAA Tournament. In their first-round game against

Lisa Leslie launches a jump shot over the outstretched arm of a defending opponent.

Portland, the Trojans allowed their 10-point lead to be slashed to two with 15 minutes to play before they regained control to win 77–62. In the second round, they led George Washington by 13 points at halftime, then fell behind by two points with 1:16 left to play before squeaking out a 76–72 victory.

In their third game, the Trojans took a commanding 45–30 halftime lead over Virginia. Once again, USC's lead slipped away as the Cavaliers went on a 17–2 run in the second half to close to within two points. But the Trojans rallied to take control and win in a rout, 85–66. "We've been in every type of situation, so we can respond to any situation," Leslie explained afterward. "I think we were very confident. We feel we're going to win, no matter what."[13]

The Trojans were one victory away from a trip to the prestigious Final Four. Standing in their way were the Louisiana Tech Lady Techsters, a gritty team that had won 23 straight games. With 4,704 fans watching at the Bud Walton Arena in Fayetteville, Arkansas, and a national television audience tuned in, the Trojans and Lady Techsters traded baskets. The game was tied 12 times in the first half until USC broke through to take a 37–34 halftime lead. Leslie and teammate Nicky McCrimmon hit baskets to open the second half to stake the Trojans to a seven-point lead.

But when Tech's Amy Brown hit a fadeaway 18-footer and a free throw, it gave her team a 55–54 lead that it never would surrender. Louisiana Tech pulled away to win the game 75–66. As the Lady Techsters jumped around the court in celebration, Leslie and her teammates walked off the court looking straight ahead and entered a cold hallway leading to their locker room. They had fought hard, and they would not hang their heads.

> "Lisa Leslie showed why she is the best player out there."
>
> —Head Coach Cheryl Miller

Leslie finished with a game-high 24 points, along with 10 rebounds, 5 blocked shots, and 2 assists. She praised the Lady Techsters afterward. "They gave a lot of second effort," Leslie said. "Second effort wins games. They are a scrappy team."[14]

When Leslie's college totals were counted, she had amassed more points (2,414), rebounds (1,214), and blocked shots (321) than any women's player in the Pac-10 Conference in history. She was a unanimous choice as the Naismith Player of the Year. She refused to be daunted by not winning the national title.

"I believe I will be a successful person, basketball or not," said Leslie. "If I don't have a national championship under my belt, I won't believe that I wasn't a successful person at USC."[15]

Lisa Leslie would not have to wait very long to experience the thrill of being a basketball champion.

5

ACHIEVING NEW DREAMS

W hen Leslie graduated from USC, there was no professional women's basketball league in the United States. Leslie had to make a decision. Should she continue playing basketball, or should she pursue another line of work? Before she had decided, she was chosen to play on the United States national team at the 1994 Goodwill Games in Atlanta, Georgia. She was clearly the best player on the court, making more than 70 percent of her shots from the floor to lead the American team in scoring at 19 points per game. The United States swept its four games to win the gold medal.

Leslie knew that some European countries had

Lisa Leslie was proud to represent the United States in international competition after finishing her college career at USC.

professional leagues. If she wanted to continue playing basketball, she would have to live overseas. When an Italian pro league in Alcamo, Italy, offered Leslie a contract to play, she could not resist. She loved basketball, and she wanted to keep playing. She accepted an offer to play for the Sicilgesso team.

Living in Italy was quite different from living in America. Other women players from the United States had a difficult time adjusting. Not Leslie. She had great fun. She enjoyed the food and the crazy-loud crowds at the games. She even learned to speak Italian. "I think a lot of American players who go overseas don't try to adapt to the other culture," Leslie said. "They seclude themselves and have their American videotapes and music sent over."[1] The Italian culture was different, but not the basketball. On the court, Leslie was a star. She averaged 22 points and 11.7 rebounds a game for Sicilgesso.

When Leslie returned home from her season in Italy, she was delighted to learn that Olympic coach Tara VanDerveer had invited her to attend team try-outs. The team would train together for one year and then compete in the 1996 Olympic Games. Each player would be paid about $50,000. The team would be called the Women's Dream Team. Fifty-six of the best women players in the United States tried out for

Lisa Leslie shoots over the Brazilian team's defenders during the gold medal game of the Olympics in Atlanta, Georgia, on August 4, 1996.

the team. After several practices and games, that number was reduced to twenty. Leslie was among the twenty. The tryouts continued. Only the best eleven players would make the team.

Finally, when the coaches had made their decision on the final roster, each hopeful player was called, one at a time, into a room where they were told whether they were kept or cut. "I went in," Leslie recalled, "and they said, 'Lisa, congratulations.' I just shouted 'Yeah!'"[2]

The team began practicing, and it was clear from the start that Leslie belonged. "Lisa will one day be the best player in the world," said teammate Dawn Staley.[3] For the next fourteen months, Leslie and her teammates traveled around the world, playing games against other national teams in countries such as Russia, Germany, China, and Japan. They ended up flying a total of 102,245 miles. They played 52 games. They won them all! Up next: the Olympic Games.

In the meantime, Leslie began working as a runway model in her spare time. She signed a deal with Wilhelmina, a major modeling agency. The agency called her "a celebrity turned supermodel."[4] She modeled evening gowns and sports gear for such magazines as *Vogue* and *TV Guide*. "At first, some of the fashion people didn't know what to think of me," Leslie recalled. "Because I'm so tall, their impression was that I would not fit into the sample sizes made for shorter women. I knew I could, so I just tried the clothes on. Everyone was so amazed!"[5]

As Leslie began walking on runways and modeling clothing, she soon learned that working with other models was not like playing on a basketball team. Models often do not talk to one another. Some are jealous of others. Leslie did not let such behavior affect her. "I talk to everybody," she said. "And I won't even take that dumb-model treatment. I'm very intelligent, and I know it."[6] As Leslie became more popular, people were discovering that she could do it all. She was articulate, a stylish dresser, an ambassador for basketball, and a strong role model for young women.

As the Women's Dream Team gathered in Atlanta, Georgia for the 1996 Olympics, the hot topic of discussion was a professional women's basketball league starting up in the United States. Not just one league, but two. The American Basketball League (ABL) and the Women's National Basketball Association (WNBA) were set to launch sometime after the Olympics. There appeared to be a future in basketball in America for Leslie and her basketball

The U.S. Women's basketball team stands for the playing of the national anthem after winning the gold medal in 1996.

friends, after all. First, though, was the important business at hand: the Games themselves.

Though the U.S. team had swept through its opponents on its world tour, victory in the Olympics was no sure thing. The U.S. team had lost in the 1992 Olympics to the Unified Team. It had lost in the 1994 World Championships to Brazil. Though the Americans had "home-court advantage" this time, they could not afford to play poorly even once against dangerous opponents.

Sure enough, with Leslie leading the way, the Women's Dream Team cruised to the gold-medal game by defeating the national teams of Cuba, Ukraine, Zaire, Australia, South Korea, and Japan. In the game against Japan, Leslie scored 35 points—the most points ever scored by an American woman in the Olympics. Against the Australians, Leslie almost single-handedly carried the U.S. team to victory. After the Australians took a 16–8 lead, Leslie seized control of the contest by leading her side on a 15–0 run. She played stout defense and finished with 22 points and 13 rebounds as the Americans rolled to a 93–71 win.

Leslie's team met powerhouse Brazil in the gold-medal game. The Brazilians had knocked out the Americans two years earlier in the World

Lisa Leslie proudly displays her gold medal.

Championships, and they won the Olympics in 1992. Brazil was led by mighty center Marta de Souza Sobral. At first, Leslie struggled guarding Sobral. Coach VanDerveer pulled Leslie from the game. Veteran player Teresa Evans gave Leslie a pep talk on the bench. Leslie went back onto the court and played harder than she ever had before. She was able to contain Sobral from then on.

On offense, coach VanDerveer devised a smart game plan in which Leslie played farther from the basket on offense to draw Sobral out with her. This created space for Leslie's teammates to cut inside for layups. Sobral was unable to guard Leslie and clog the lane at the same time. When Sobral was away from the basket, players like Dawn Staley were free to streak to the hoop. When Sobral strayed from Leslie to try to help more inside, Leslie drilled open jumpers. She hit 12 of 14 shots in the game and finished with 29 points. The U.S. team pulled away in the second half to win easily, 111–87. They had scored more points in an Olympic final than any other team in history.

Leslie cried with joy as she stood atop the victory stand with her teammates. They held hands and

> With Lisa Leslie leading the way, the women's team cruised to the gold-medal game.

raised them high as the crowd cheered. Tears streamed down Leslie's face as her gold medal was draped around her neck. "We accomplished what we set out to do," Leslie said. "We tried to get women's basketball to the next level. Our game speaks for itself."[7]

6

"WE GOT NEXT"

The American Basketball League (ABL) opened play in 1996. Several of Leslie's Olympic teammates played for the ABL. Not Leslie. She wanted to wait for what she thought would be a stronger league—the Women's National Basketball Association (WNBA). Leslie proved to be a prophet. Because of poor planning and financial struggles, the ABL lasted just three seasons before folding. In contrast, the WNBA has been going strong since its beginning.

Olympic team members Sheryl Swoopes and Rebecca Lobo were the first two players signed by the WNBA. Leslie was third. In December 1996, she inked a contract at a press conference in Los Angeles.

Lisa Leslie shoots over Rebecca Lobo of the New York Liberty during a game at the Great Western Forum in Inglewood, California, on June 21, 1997.

Afterward, she got a big hug from her mother. The following month, she became a member of the Los Angeles Sparks, one of the league's eight original teams.

On June 21, 1997, the WNBA opened its inaugural season with the slogan "We Got Next." It meant that now it was the women's turn to play. The opening game pitted Leslie's Sparks against Lobo's New York Liberty. With a Los Angeles Forum crowd of 14,284 and a national TV audience watching, Leslie's team fell 67–57 to the Liberty. The Sparks had only a week of practice to prepare, and it showed.

Dressed in purple and gold, just like the Lakers who played in the same arena, the Sparks committed 25 turnovers. They took an 8–4 lead after four minutes on a short jumper by Leslie, but the Liberty went on an 8–2 run to take the lead and never trailed again. Lobo led the winners with 16 points. Leslie matched that with 16 of her own to lead the Sparks. But she was not satisfied. "I'm happy I got it over with because I don't feel like I played well at all," she said.[1]

As the season unfolded, Leslie clearly was her team's leader. But the Sparks struggled. Six weeks after the season-opener, the Sparks were floundering with an 8–12 record, while the Liberty were out in front at 15–4. The teams met again, this time at Madison Square Garden in New York. Paced by a stirring defensive performance from Leslie, the Sparks shocked the Liberty 67–50. Leslie scored 10 points and grabbed a game-high 14 rebounds. More impressive, she forced Lobo, New York's leading scorer, into her worst shooting night of the season. Lobo made just 2 of 14 shots from the floor to finish with 4 points.

The Sparks made a push for the playoffs but came up short, finishing with a 14–14 record. Leslie led the league in rebounding (9.5 rebounds per game), finished second in blocked shots (2.1 blocks), and was third in scoring (15.9 points per game). Still, she blamed herself for her team's failure to reach the playoffs. She said her steady modeling work before the season started left her little time to stay in top basketball condition. "I just was not prepared to play basketball, and I underestimated what level the WNBA would be at."[2]

Leslie vowed to improve. She began an intense weight-training program to bulk up. She hired a personal trainer to help her improve on the fundamentals of the game. She practiced at UCLA four times a week. Eventually she added 15 pounds of muscle to her slight frame. Whenever she was not working out, she was modeling. She was

Whenever she is not playing or training for basketball, Leslie is usually working as a model.

making commercials and appearing in magazine advertisements for such big companies as General Motors, Sears, American Express, Lawry's, Anne Klein, and Nike. "I like to show girls that you can be tough and feminine, too," she said.[3]

Leslie started the 1998 season with great enthusiasm. Coach Julie Rosseau said, "She's willing to take this team on her back and carry us on her shoulders. We'll ride."[4] As the season wore on, she became fast friends with Lakers center Shaquille O'Neal. "Lisa has an incredible drive to win," said O'Neal. "She hates to lose, even during a pickup game."[5]

Unfortunately for Leslie, her team lost more than it won, finishing the season with a disappointing 12–18 record. But the winning was about to begin. In the 1999 season opener, Leslie scored 19 points to lead her team past the Sacramento Monarchs. Two days later, she equaled her pro career point total with 30, and added 19 rebounds in a dominating 91–59 victory over the Cleveland Rockers. After trading wins and losses over the next two weeks, the Sparks won six games in a row. They dropped two, and then won six straight again. They were headed to the playoffs. First, though, the WNBA staged its first-ever All-Star Game.

In front of a sellout crowd of 18,649 at Madison

Lisa Leslie wrestles a rebound away from Jessie Hicks of the Utah Starzz.

Square Garden, Leslie and her Western Conference teammates put on a dazzling show. The West, led by Leslie's strong moves to the basket, jumped out to leads of 10–0 and 17–2. The East never had a chance.

The West breezed to a 79–61 win. Leslie scored 13 points and grabbed 5 rebounds and was named the game's Most Valuable Player. "I guess," she said, "I'm going to be a part of history, being the first MVP."[6]

> "I'm going to be a part of history, being the first [All-Star] MVP."
>
> —Lisa Leslie

The regular season resumed, and the Sparks wound up with a 20–12 record, second-best in the league. Their opponent in the first round of the play-offs was their nemesis, the Monarchs, who finished just a single game behind them in the standings. The first round was a single-elimination game, meaning the winner would advance and the loser's season would be over. The Sparks appeared doomed after they scored just 9 baskets in the first half to trail at the break, 32–21. But Leslie rallied her teammates in the second half. They went on a 17–6 run to tie the game at 38. An 11–4 run later in the half put the Sparks ahead by seven. They cruised home with a 71–58 win.

The Sparks next faced the mighty Houston

Comets in the second round. It was a best-of-three series, with the first game in Los Angeles and the next two in Houston. The Comets had won the first two WNBA titles and owned the best record again in 1999. But Leslie was not intimidated. After the Sparks fell behind 8–0, Leslie scored on a layup to get her team on the board. Midway through the first half, Leslie and Tamecka Dixon combined to score eight straight points to give their team its first lead. When Houston pulled ahead 27–26, Leslie drilled a three-pointer, and the Sparks never trailed again. They rolled to a 75–60 victory, with Leslie leading all scorers with 23 points.

The Comets showed why they were champions by pummeling the Sparks 83–55 in the second game. The Sparks refused to quit. Midway through the second half of the final game, they had the lead 53–49, but the Comets ripped off seven straight points to seize control. A basket by Leslie pulled Los Angeles to within 61–59, but the Comets distanced themselves down the stretch to win 72–62. Afterward, Leslie told reporters: "I think that this Comets team knows that they just went through the best team in the WNBA."[7]

The 2000 season was a near repeat. With new coach Michael Cooper designing plays and Leslie

Leslie tries to get past the Houston Comets' Tina Thompson during a game at the Summit in Houston, Texas.

dominating inside, the Sparks rolled to an incredible 28–4 record. Along the way, Leslie became the first player in league history to earn Player of the Week honors three times. During one stretch, she hit 49 straight free throws. The Sparks met the Comets in the Western Conference Finals once again. The Comets won the first game in Houston and then came to Los Angeles to eliminate the Sparks with a 74–69 victory. The Comets would go on to win their fourth straight WNBA championship. Would Leslie and the Sparks ever break through?

Leslie took time off from the Sparks to represent the United States in the 2000 Olympic Games. Coach Nell Fortner described Leslie as a player who would "take your head off."[8] With Leslie out front, the Americans rolled to the gold medal in Sydney, Australia. But Leslie's joy soon turned to sorrow. In December, she learned that her stepfather of five years, Tom Espinoza, had liver cancer. She had just bought Tom and her mother, Christine, a new house in Los Angeles six months earlier. Lisa came to the house every day to offer comfort and support. One month later, Tom died. Lisa grieved with her mother. Her inner strength grew, and she dedicated herself to winning the WNBA championship.

7

CENTER OF ATTENTION

Leslie had been writing a list of her personal goals every year since she became a pro. She called this list her "Mission Statement." Each year this document was about one page long. But before the 2001 season, she typed up a three-page "to-do" list. One of the sentences said this: "I'm going to be MVP and lead the Sparks to their first championship."[1]

This is just what she did. With focus and determination, Leslie led the Sparks to the playoffs once again. Along the way, her teammates saw a changed woman. "She used to be feminine and dainty when she ran, like she didn't want anyone to hear her," said forward DeLisha Milton. "Now she almost stomps.

Leslie attempts a free throw during Game 2 of the WNBA Finals against the New York Liberty on August 31, 2002.

She wants the other team to hear her coming."[2] Leslie won her second MVP award in the All-Star Game, but she wanted something more.

The Sparks played seven games in the playoffs. They won six. First, they finally got past the Comets, winning by 5 and 12 points. Next, they beat the Monarchs in three games, advancing to the finals with a 93–62 victory. Finally, they swept the Charlotte Sting, winning the title with an 82–54 triumph. Leslie scored 24 points in each of the two final-round games. Amid the wild celebration at the Staples Center in downtown Los Angeles, she held the crystal Tiffany trophy aloft as confetti rained down. Leslie became the first woman in WNBA history to be named MVP of the regular season, the playoffs, and the All-Star Game. "Lisa was not going to be denied this year," said Coach Cooper. "It's like she's been on a mission since the beginning of the season."[3]

Leslie had become the most dominant force in the WNBA. She showed her greatness again in 2002 by leading the Sparks to another title. This time, they swept the New York Liberty in the finals. The season was marked by her third All-Star Game MVP and her first official dunk in a game. It happened at the Staples Center against the Miami Sol. With 4:44 left in the first half, she caught a pass, took two steps, and threw down a thunderous right-hand jam. "I wasn't thinking," said Leslie. "I just turned around, and I was free."[4]

The 2003 season was nearly identical. The Sparks sailed into the playoffs and reached the finals for the third straight year. But their hopes for a three-peat were dashed by the Detroit Shock. After winning the opener, the Sparks lost two straight in Detroit to relinquish the crown. The setback simply made Leslie rededicate herself.

The Sparks charged out in 2004 with Leslie leading the way. Midway through the season, Los Angeles had the WNBA's best record at 19–7. Leslie was among the league's leaders in scoring at 16 points per game, and her average of 10 rebounds and 2.9 blocks ranked first. The season was interrupted for more than two weeks for the 2004 Olympic Games, which were staged in Athens, Greece. Leslie was named the starting center for Team USA.

The Americans had won seventeen straight Olympic contests and the last two gold medals, and were clear favorites to win it all again. They were loaded with talented players, but everyone knew Leslie was the key to victory. "No one is going to do the things Lisa Leslie does inside, outside,

Lisa Leslie battles Ticha Penicheiro of the Sacramento Monarchs for a loose ball.

rebounding, blocking," said team Dawn Staley. "She's just a force. She's the best player in the world."[5]

After cruising to easy wins in its first two games, Team USA held just a seven-point lead at halftime against South Korea. Leslie had scored 13 points, but she knew she had to do more. Playing inside against the shorter South Korean team, Leslie squeezed between double-teams to score 11 points in the third quarter, as the Americans went on a 22–2 run to pull away. They won easily, 80-57, with Leslie finishing with a game-high 25 points. "Why do you think I call her the Big Dog?" said Team USA coach Van Chancellor. "Because when the time comes, the big dog will hunt, partner."[6]

Team USA won three more times to reach the semifinals. They had won their six games by an average of 29 points. But the contest against Russia came down to the final moments. Team USA was ahead by a basket, 60–58, when Sheryl Swoopes hit a jumper from the left side with 3:54 remaining. She followed with another basket to put the Americans up by six. Then Leslie fed Tina Thompson for a layup to make it 66–58 with 2:50 to go. The Americans would not score again, but it was enough, as they held on for a 66–62 triumph. "We just weathered the storm,"

Leslie said. "We showed a lot of heart and stayed together."[7]

In the gold medal game the following night, Team USA rolled to a 74–63 victory over Australia. Staley scored 14 points and Leslie added 13 to lead the team. When the final buzzer sounded, Leslie and her teammates grabbed a huge American flag and skipped around the court with it, laughing and crying. American fans in the stands chanted "U-S-A, U-S-A." Leslie had won her third Olympic gold medal. No American woman has ever won more in basketball.

Leslie does it all. One day she is on a playground in New York, filming an advertisement for basketball shoes. The next day she is going to the Supreme Court to meet Justices Sandra Day O'Connor and Ruth Bader Ginsburg. She does color commentary for USC basketball games and reports for *NBA Inside Stuff*. She has appeared as a guest actor on television shows like *Hang Time* and *Moesha*. She has also appeared on game shows such as *Who Wants to be a Millionaire?* and *The Weakest Link*. She is a spokesperson for Big Brothers Big Sisters of America, a charity that helps children. She became certified in cardiopulmonary resuscitation (CPR) in

> "Focus is what has enabled me to excel in life."
> —Lisa Leslie

Lisa Leslie triumphantly hoists her 2001 Finals MVP trophy above her head.

order to host foster children at her home. And, of course, she is a pro basketball player and a model.

How does she do it?

"It's all about focus," Leslie explains. "Focus is what has enabled me to excel in life. When I play basketball, there is absolutely nothing else on my mind. When I'm modeling, I'm focused on modeling and doing the best I can for the photographer or audience. When I'm a special correspondent for *NBA Inside Stuff*, I'm totally focused on what I need to do to give the best interview possible."[8]

Leslie is rich and famous. In 2003, she played basketball for $325,000 and earned more than $1 million more in endorsements. Her Mercedes Benz bears the license plate "LLWNBA." She serves as a spokesperson for the league and a role model for children. "Whether I'm on the court or the runway, I'm out there entertaining," she says. "I'm passionate about both. I'm doing what I love with attitude and style. The point is, I am a woman, always."[9]

Leslie's fortitude is immense. But without opportunity, such passion and drive can go unnoticed. Above all, Leslie understands the value of sports. "Because of sports," she says, "I've been around the world."[10]

CHAPTER NOTES

Chapter I. A Champion

1. Staff Report, "The Hard Road," Associated Press, September 8, 2003.
2. Staff Report, "Are Sparks the Underdogs?" Associated Press, September 12, 2003.
3. Pam Lambert, "Woman Warrior," *People*, June 30, 1997, p. 109.
4. Staff Report, "Leslie Leads Way as Sparks Coast to Win," Associated Press, September 12, 2003, p. 109.
5. Jeff Savage, *Top 10 Women's Basketball Stars* (Berkeley Heights, N.J.: Enslow Publishers, Inc., 2001), p. 20.
6. Lambert, p. 109.

Chapter 2. Growing Up Fast

1. Pamela Lewis, "Shooting for the Moon," *Basketball Digest*, June 29, 1998, p. 28.
2. Melissa King, "Lisa Leslie as a Work in Progress," *Sports Illustrated Women*, May/June 2002, p. 86.
3. Pam Lambert, "Woman Warrior," *People*, June 30, 1997, p. 109.
4. Ibid.
5. Lewis, p. 28.
6. Lambert, p. 109.
7. King, p. 86.

8. Bob Der, "Ask the Athletes," *Sports Illustrated for Kids*, April 1997, p. 13.

9. Maya Browne, "Shapely, Sexy, Strong," *Heart & Soul*, June/July 1997, p. 44.

Chapter 3. Learning the Game

1. Melissa King, "Lisa Leslie as a Work in Progress," *Sports Illustrated Women*, May/June 2002, p. 86.

2. Ibid.

3. Brian Landman, "Trying Out for National Team Gives Young Star New Viewpoint," *St. Petersburg Times*, June 16, 1990, p. 5.

4. Staff Report, "The First Ladies of Hoops," *Ebony*, March 1998, p. 98.

5. Landman, p. 5.

6. Bob Der, "Ask the Athletes," *Sports Illustrated for Kids*, December 1996, p. 13.

7. Mark Stewart, *Lisa Leslie—Queen of the Court* (New York: Children's Press, 1998), p. 14.

8. Jake Curtis, "USC Freshman Leslie Living Up to Her High School Reputation," *San Francisco Chronicle*, December 7, 1990, p. 1.

9. Ibid.

10. Stewart, p.19.

11. Landman, p. 5.

Chapter 4. Record Breaker

1. Mike Mulligan, "USC's Leslie Brings Dunk, Lots of Hype to Town," *Chicago Sun Times*, November 30, 1990, p. 1.

2. Brian Landman, "Trying Out For National Team Gives Young Star New Viewpoint," *St. Petersburg Times*, June 16, 1990, p. 5.

3. Pete Thomas, "Leslie Puts Trojans on Higher Level," *Los Angeles Times*, November 23, 1990, p. 3.

4. Ibid.

5. Landman, p. 5.

6. Mel Greenberg, "At USC, a Cheryl Miller in the Making?" *Philadelphia Inquirer*, November 27, 1990, p. 5.

7. Mulligan, p. 1.

8. Ibid.

9. Tony Cooper, "Stanford Women Top USC," *San Francisco Chronicle*, January 17, 1992, p. 3.

10. Lisa Nahus Saxon, "USC Women Knock Off 3rd-Ranked Stanford," *Riverside Press Enterprise*, January 19, 1993.

11. Press release, USC Sports Information, January 30, 1994.

12. Ibid.

13. Jim Short, "USC Women 1 Away From Final Four," *Riverside Press Enterprise*, p. 4.

14. Jerry L. Reed, "Louisiana Tech Wins Mideast Region Crown," *Northwest Arkansas Times*, March 27, 1994, p. 3.

15. Jim Short, "USC Hands Over Hopes," *Riverside Press Enterprise*, March 27, 1994, p. 1.

Chapter 5. Achieving New Dreams

1. Ross Atkin, "On the Court or Off, She's Still in Vogue," *Christian Science Monitor*, July 26, 1996, p. 12.

2. Mark Stewart, *Lisa Leslie—Queen of the Court* (New York: Children's Press, 1998), p. 3.

3. Atkin, p. 12.

4. Anna Seaton Huntington, "So I Wanna Be a Superstar," *Women's Sports & Fitness*, November/December 1996, p. 50.
5. Maya Browne, "Shapely, Sexy, Strong," *Heart & Soul*, June/July 1997, p. 44.
6. Brent Kelley, *Lisa Leslie* (Philadelphia: Chelsea House, 2001), pp. 30–31.
7. Ibid., p. 39.

Chapter 6. "We Got Next"

1. Pamela Lewis, "N.Y. Wins WNBA Tipoff, 67–57," *Long Beach Press-Telegram*, June 22, 1997, p. 1.
2. Pamela Lewis, "Shooting for the Moon," *Basketball Digest*, June 29, 1998, p. 28.
3. Brent Kelley, *Lisa Leslie* (Philadelphia: Chelsea House, 2001), pp. 30–31.
4. Lewis, p. 28.
5. Pam Lambert, "Woman Warrior," *People*, June 30, 1997, p. 109.
6. Kelley, p. 13.
7. Kevin Ding, "Taunting Too Much for Leslie to Take," *Orange County Register*, August 31, 1999, p. 1.
8. Melissa King, "Lisa Leslie as a Work in Progress," *Sports Illustrated Women*, May/June 2002, p. 86.

Chapter 7. Center of Attention

1. Melissa King, "Lisa Leslie as a Work in Progress," *Sports Illustrated Women*, May/June 2002, p. 86.
2. Kelli Anderson, "Woman Possessed," *Sports Illustrated*, September 10, 2001, p. 29.
3. Ibid.
4. Benjamin Nugent, "Leslie's Historic Jam Session," *Time Europe*, August 12, 2002, p. 60.

5. Sherry Skalko, "Leslie Still Team USA's Leader, Star," *ESPN.com*, n.d., <http://www.espn.com/> August 18, 2004.

6. Ibid.

7. Staff, "Swoopes' Late Heroics Hold Off Russia," Associated Press, August 27, 2004.

8. Brent Kelley, *Lisa Leslie* (Philadelphia: Chelsea House, 2001), p. 56.

9. Anna Seaton Huntington, "So I Wanna Be a Superstar," *Women's Sports & Fitness*, November/ December 1996, p. 50.

10. Ross Atkin, "On the Court or Off, She's Still in Vogue," *Christian Science Monitor*, July 26, 1996, p. 12.

CAREER STATISTICS

COLLEGE

Season	Team	GP	FG%	REB	AST	STL	BLK	PTS	PPG
1991–92	USC	30	.478	299	20	43	78	582	19.4
1992–93	USC	31	.550	261	46	56	54	632	20.4
1993–94	USC	29	.558	285	59	60	95	543	18.7
1994–95	USC	30	.558	369	83	69	94	657	21.9
TOTALS		120	.534	1,214	208	228	321	2,414	20.1

GP—Games Played
FG%—Field Goal Percentage

REB—Rebounds
AST—Assists
STL—Steals

BLK—Blocks
PTS—Points
PPG—Points Per Game

WNBA

Season	Team	GP	FG%	REB	AST	STL	BLK	PTS	PPG
1997	L.A.	28	.431	266	74	39	59	445	15.9
1998	L.A.	28	.478	285	70	42	60	549	19.6
1999	L.A.	32	.468	248	56	36	49	500	15.6
2000	L.A.	32	.458	306	60	31	74	570	17.8
2001	L.A.	31	.473	298	73	34	71	606	19.5
2002	L.A.	31	.466	322	83	46	90	523	16.9
2003	L.A.	23	.442	231	46	31	63	424	18.4
2004	L.A.	34	.494	336	88	50	98	598	17.6
TOTALS		239	.465	2,292	550	309	564	4,215	17.6

GP—Games Played
FG%—Field Goal Percentage
REB—Rebounds
AST—Assists
STL—Steals
BLK—Blocks
PTS—Points
PPG—Points Per Game

WHERE
TO WRITE

Ms. Lisa Leslie
c/o The Staples Center
1111 S. Figueroa Street
Los Angeles, CA 90015

INTERNET ADDRESSES

WNBA.com

http://www.wnba.com/

Lisa Leslie Player Info

http://www.wnba.com/playerfile/lisa_leslie/index.
html?nav=page

INDEX